MY 1ST BO

MILITARY SUPERHEROES

★★★★★

Sara Kale

Rainbow Arts Studio
Copyright © 2022 Sara Kale
All Rights Reserved

Amazon Page: amazon.com/author/sarakale
Email: sara.rainbowartsstudio@gmail.com
IG: rainbow_artsstudio

United States Armed Forces

★ ★ ★ ★ ★

The United States Armed Forces are the military forces of the United States. The Armed Forces consists of six service branches.

US Armed Forces Branches

★ ★ ★ ★ ★

United States Army

United States Navy

United States Marine Corps

United States Air Force

United States Coast Guard

United States Space Force

Commander in Chief

★ ★ ★ ★ ★

The President of the
United States is the
Commander in Chief
of the
U.S. Armed Forces.

U.S. ARMY

★ ★ ★ ★ ★

The U.S. Army is a land fighting force. The Army protects our country against the outside threats and preserves peace. The members of the Army are called "**Soldiers**".

U.S. NAVY

★ ★ ★ ★ ★

The U.S. Navy is a fighting force at sea. The Navy keeps the oceans safe for travel and trade. The members of the Navy are called "Sailors".

U.S. MARINE CORPS

★ ★ ★ ★ ★

The U.S. Marine Corps provides first response for missions on land, sea and in air. The members of the Marine Corps are called "Marines".

U.S. Airforce

★ ★ ★ ★ ★

The U.S. Airforce is a fighting force in the air. The Airforce conducts air operations and provides air support for Army and Navy. The members of the Airforce are called "Airmen".

U.S. COAST GUARD

★ ★ ★ ★ ★

The U.S. Coast Guard safeguards and maintains our country's waterways (seas, ports, rivers, lakes, etc.). The members of the Coast Guard are called **"Coast Guardsman"**.

U.S. Space Force

★ ★ ★ ★ ★

The U.S. Space Force defends our country and freedom to operate in space. The members of the Space Force are called **"Guardians"**. The Guardians launch rockets, put satellites into space and also operate those satellites.

K-9 CORPS

★ ★ ★ ★ ★

The U.S. military working dogs are highly skilled warriors, trained by the best handlers or soldiers. About 1,600 military working dogs help with missions spanning land, air and sea to keep our nation safe.

Honoring Our Military

★ ★ ★ ★ ★

We honor, celebrate and appreciate our Military for their service and sacrifice by observing :

Armed Forces Day

Memorial Day

Veterans Day

Made in the USA
Las Vegas, NV
27 October 2024